The BC 3000 - A

One sunny day in August, I set out on an adventure, an adventure that would see me ride over 3,000 miles around the coast of the British mainland on a 125cc motorcycle, in 10 days. To put that into context of distance, it would be the same as travelling by road from England via France, Germany, Austria, Hungary, Romania, Serbia, Bulgaria, Turkey, Syria to Baghdad in Iraq, something that may well have been worth considering before I left. Ignorance is bliss, until the blister!

It all started on one grubby mid-winter weekend when I was out on my motorcycle, with no destination in mind. I was just riding to shake off the week and to feel the freedom, but as I rode, I realised that I wasn't shaking off the week, I was getting frustrated with the humdrum of life and the monotony of work. It was making me restless and it was giving me seriously itchy feet, and not in a sporting way! I knew I had to get away, had to test myself with some sort of challenge.

Each year, I push myself to complete a challenge and go on an adventure. The previous year, I had canoed the length of the River Thames from the source to the sea, taking my 15 year old son with me, in my ongoing quest to make him expedition ready!

I spent months planning it in detail, studying the waterways, calculating suitable campsite locations, measuring distances and rates, pre booking everything as I went. Only I overlooked one small but incredibly important fact - the inflatable canoe that could be packed down to fit into a back pack that we took with us was not at all like the rigid plastic one that we had trained with. For the entire journey, we had to paddle nearly twice as much and the whole thing spiralled into something that was tantamount to working on a chain gang. Our 'adventure' turned into something that was ruthless and gruelling and we toiled day-in, day-out, pushing ourselves so hard to make our pre-booked destinations on time. It was something that I quietly lapped up as "all part of the challenge", but in truth, it was a trip that has probably burnt the fear of a paddle into my son's soul for the rest of his life.

I should also mention here, the psychological effects that I inflicted on the boy and my girlfriend, the year before that, when hit by hurricane force winds whilst mountaineering in Snowdonia; him splayed out like a starfish, clinging on to the side of the mountain with sheer terror in his eyes or the memories that he will cherish forever of a mid-February spent walking the length of the Suffolk coast and wild camping in minus 5 degrees!

So this year, I had a hunch that things were going to be different and my boy would not be by my side for this one. Now aged 17 and at the mercy of his raging hormones, he was "in love" and even 24 hours away from his girlfriend would clearly result in death or a far worse fate, so I didn't push it. My girlfriend, knowing me much better than I care to admit, is far too wily to come with me, but is always extremely supportive in getting rid of me for a few weeks!

A few friends had shown an interest in doing a trip with me, but I decided to take the opportunity to undertake a solo adventure. It would give me the opportunity to travel alone, to reconnect and remind myself who I am, not a colleague, a friend or relation, but this would allow me to simply just be me.

The next day, I rolled the bike out again. It was Sunday, I had nowhere to be and I was certainly going to make the most of it. I rode with no particular destination in mind, I just rode; down the hedge-lined winding Suffolk roads and through the picturesque villages. Looping through Lavenham, an ancient village full of half timbered medieval cottages and a 15th century church, all dramatically framed under a particularly moody December sky.

I rode at no pace and with no purpose, riding only for the joy of it and as I rode, my mind turned to the possibilities of the trip to come. I was almost drooling at the thought of the freedom and the adventure. Just then, the heavens conspired against me and the first pellets of rain started to spit down on me, hitting my visor like rusty nails. As the sky blackened and the clouds twisted, I wound open the throttle and headed for cover pulling into a little market town and the nearest pub; a part of dreary sticky-carpeted chain serving cheap beer and food. As I swung in to the car park, the skies opened and the rain battered down on me, I dashed in to the pub, pulling off my helmet and gloves and headed straight for an empty table that was set perfectly in front of a freshly lit fire. I hung my dripping jacket on a chair and pushed it slightly closer to the fire, placed my gloves on top and rested my helmet on the table like a flag to claim my table and headed for the bar to order a coffee and a bowl of chips.

I returned to the table with my steaming mug of hot coffee and sat to ponder my options a little more whilst waiting for my chips to arrive. As I sat waiting, I gazed across the pub to a cluster of lost souls, the same cluster that seem to gather like leaves in the corner of each of the chain's pubs.

They all stood facing the bar and with a cheer, they all toasted in unison, tipping their glasses towards a wreath that rested at the end of the bar. Nestled within the wreath, was a picture of one of their recently fallen comrades. "Dave" they all cheer in unison, the glasses chinked between them and to my astonishment, they ironically toasted each other's health and fell back into their chairs.

With that, the barmaid carved her way across the room with my bowl of chips and just as she placed them down, there was a crash, followed by roar of laughter. I looked over and to my surprise, one of the congregation had tipped off the back of his chair and lay flat on his back, still in his chair, with his arm held out straight to the sky, still brandishing his half-full pint glass of beer, this was immediately followed by a second wave of cheering. The barmaid glared over to the crowd, looked back at me saying "sorry" and "enjoy your food". She rolled her eyes, turned and headed off to scold the noisy revellers, leaving me to my chips and to return to ploughing the depths of my mind to plan my next adventure, before life enticed me to became the one of the pub's congregation or even worse, the next Dave!

As I sat there, I ravenously thought of all the exotic countries that I was desperate to travel in; mountains that I wanted to stand aloft on; dangerous roads that I wanted to ride, anything not to waste my life and then, in a sudden flash, I thought back to a childhood dream, a dream I had to ride a Honda C90 on the Silk Road to India. As quickly as it had sprung to mind, another thought came flashing in and my dream was immediately shattered as I tumbled back down to earth remembering I had a family, bills and only a couple of weeks available for me to travel in!

My mind poured again, then it struck me - what

about this fair country? I could ride down to Land's End and then up to John O' Groats. There was so much more of the UK that I wanted to see and if I was going to do that, I may as well do it all. I would ride the coast of Britain, but to make it more epic, I would do it on my Chinese 125cc. "Perfect", I thought, my mind was set and my chips gone. I refilled my coffee cup and immediately started to outline my plan.

I would leave my home, near Ipswich in Suffolk on the east coast and ride south, keeping the sea to my left in order to prevent oncoming cars from inter-rupting my view of it. This would also give me the added advantage of avoiding yo-yoing up and down on dead end roads.

I would aim to sleep in the larger coastal towns overnight, places with a pulse that would give me plenty of accommodation options and offer some hustle and bustle around me to compensate for any days that might leave me feeling isolated from the long days on the road. Places with a good few food vendors to give me lots of food options and a petrol station, so that I could fill my motorbike up with fuel every morning ready for the day ahead.

I would take a lightweight tent; my Colman Cobra, a tent that I have had for years, weighs in at just over 2kg and pitches in just a few minutes. Its only down-side is that it is a very low tent, great for high winds but not so good for sitting up in and sorting out gear when the rain is pouring outside. It makes me feel a bit like Dracula trying to sort his washing out at midday! However, its weight and reliability compensate above and beyond any downsides for me.

In my opinion, the biggest drawback to a tent, especially if you wild camp on the beaches on the way, is that when you get caught out in a downpour, and you will get caught in a downpour, you have to pitch the tent in the rain, try not to get the tent wet on the inside while you are soaking wet and then try to dry your clothes which is a near impossible feat. Whereas the humble campsite often has washing machines and tumble dryers and this is also true of hostels – an invaluable service which is not available at most hotels and B&Bs.

As I travel light and I mean very light, the clothes which I take with me need washing regularly. When I have to stay in a hotel or B&B whilst on my travels, I enter the shower in my pants, socks and t-shirt with my bar of soap, give them a good wash and place them on the towel rail to dry overnight. Apologies if that image gets stuck in your head now but my system works well for me!

I love a good hostel, along with the added bonus of a kitchen and a dining room, they often sell basic hot food. You can sit on a sofa in the evening and chat to like mined people, something that I particular like. One piece of essential advice would be to make sure that the hostel you book is a backpacker's hostel as some hostels in bigger cities have permanent guests, something that I first came across in Amsterdam when me and a couple of friends spent a night with rough sleepers in a converted church, we received no trouble, but it may not be everyone's cup of tea!

The route for my trip almost formed itself. As you zoom in on a map of Britain, the names of the larger coastal town pop out at you. Some of them were holiday destinations that I felt were a must visit and some of them were smaller towns and less populated and less touristy places. Some of them were Sites of Special Scientific Interest, these are some of Britain's most spectacular areas and when you remove the towns on deadend roads to take out any yoyoing up and down roads towns (Sorry yoyo towns), this leaves the most enticing route for a costal adventure with some of the best destinations that Britain has to offer.

I started with 20 main waypoints around the country that all have appeal and character of their own - Margate - Brighton - Torquay - Lands' End - Newquay - Lynton - Tenby - Aberystwyth - Liverpool- Whitehaven - Dumfries - Fort William - John O' Groats - Peterhead - Edinburgh - Berwick upon Tweed - Robin Hoods Bay - Cromer - Lowestoft - Woodbridge with Google maps set to avoid motorways and tolls.

Once I had my 20 main waypoints, I then filled in the spaces with 30 extra waypoints of interest or natural beauty always keeping in mind no long yoyoing up and down roads, making 50 waypoints in total.

Waypoints:

1. Margate
2. Dover
3. Brighton
4. Bournemouth
5. Torquay
6. Looe
7. St Austell
8. Helston
9. Land's End
10. St Ives
11. Newquay
12. Ilfracombe
13. Lynton
14. Cardiff
15. Port Talbot
16. Swansea
17. Tenby
18. Pembroke Dock
19. St David's
20. Fishguard
21. Aberystwyth
22. Llanberis
23. Liverpool
24. Blackpool
25. Kendal
26. Duddon Bridge
27. Whitehaven

28. Dumfries
29. Stranraer
30. Fort William
31. Poolewe
32. Ratagan
33. Ullapool
34. Durness
35. John O Groats
36. Inverness
37. Peterhead
38. Edinburgh
39. Berwick upon Tweed
40. Robin Hood's Bay
41. Horningsea
42. Grimsby
43. Hunstanton
44. Blakeney
45. Cromer
46. Mundesley
47. Waxham
48. Great Yarmouth
49. Lowestoft
50. Woodbridge

Total distance – 3,114 Miles

In my opinion, planning is the key to success, the people that seem to float around like free spirits are still planning, but they are just doing on a daily basis. I would recommend that you plan everything down to the smallest detail, that way when you leave and are on the road, all of the work will have been done, you will be relaxed and truly free, with your mind on the adventure ahead. There is a certain amount of sadomasochism in packing, I love doing it but it pains me. I like conjuring up far-flung scenarios in my mind, that in all honesty if they were left unchecked, I would most certainly be carrying a machete, anti-snake venom, pots and pans along with the all-important tool chest, spare parts and tyres and not forgetting the all important bear spray!

I love the containers, bags and cases with all the compartments, my mind races desperately thinking how I could fill those seductive little pockets. Then I have to pull myself back to reality and assess the journey that I am actually making, reground myself, and be a little less Golem in my decision making and a little more Buddhist, taking on a more minimalist approach and ask myself do I need this or do I just want this?

If there is less than 100% chance that I will need it, then it doesn't get packed. I love my camping stove, a must in the mountains to stave off hypothermia when miles from any civilisation, but probably not needed so desperately on the A9 with shops around every corner, however, if taking it makes the trip possible, then you must, "cut your cloth accordingly" as my mother would always say! And keeping the weight down makes the bike leaner, more efficient, better to handle all adding up to a more enjoyable to ride and enhancing the trip.

For this journey, the following items made it on to my bike:

- Motorcycle Clothing:
  - Waterproof jacket and trousers
  - Gloves x 2
  - Helmet
  - Motorcycle jacket and trousers
  - Braces (doubles up as a good washing line)
  - Touring boots
  - Neck gaiter

- Luggage:
  - Soft panniers
  - Top box
  - Cargo net, excellent for a quick stash of anything and for drying clothes

- Dry bags for:
  - Clean clothes (a dry bag with a down jacket in it makes an excellent pillow)
  - Dirty clothes
  - Documents
  - Electronics
  - Wash bag
  - Tools
  - First aid kit

- Bike maintenance and first aid (not kept together!)
    - Basics tools and cable ties
    - Pocket knife (kept in my pocket)
    - LED head torch
    - Small tin of Vaseline with aloe vera, for me and the bike
    - Pain killers
    - Antihistamine tablets
    - One bandage
    - 25 mm Gorilla tape (I use it as a plaster too)
    - Germoline, all in two dry bags and accessible at all times

- Finance and paperwork
    - Cash
    - Bank cards
    - ID
    - Tickets and booking forms, electronic copies backed up

- Technology
    - Mobile phone
    - HD action camera with spare batteries
    - Power accessories
    - Power chargers, cables
    - Headphones

- Wash kit

- Small travel Toothbrush
- Small tube of Toothpaste
- Multi-purpose soap for hair, body and clothing
- Small travel towel
- Roll-on deodorant
- Razor

- Clothing
  - Belt
  - Trousers x2 (one pair with zip off legs)
  - T-shirt x2
  - Shirt x2
  - Ultra-lightweight down jacket
  - Underwear x 3
  - Lightweight shoes

- Camping Equipment
  - Water bottle
  - Wipes
  - Short parachute cord (can be used as a clothes line too)
  - Down sleeping bag
  - Tent 2.2kg
  - Inflatable sleep mat
  - Silk sleeping bag liner
  - Spork

All of the above items were packed on to my little Zongshen RX 125, for some the thought of a Chinese motorcycle would sends shivers down the spine.

But with rising costs in the showroom and being on a mission to get more bang for my buck, I went for a Chinese machine.

As I started to look around, I was amazed by the array of Chinese bikes, on the whole copies from bikes I remember as a child, like the CG 125 and the SR 125 to only name a few, all imported, rebranded and pushed back out as the new kids on the block, or as juicy, mouth-watering brand revivals from our motorcycle manufacturing Christmas past, drawing us in with bearded retro, hipster twists and all at affordable prices.

These, the same motorcycles that they have manufactured for years on their own turf, bikes that have come full circle, and are now retro to us, models that have been sold on their homeland to provide economical, low-cost travel for the masses, that produce just enough power to propel three people in flip-flops along with a live chicken and other cringe worthy variations!

The Zongshen RX1 stood out to me with it its GS adventure bike look, cradling an engine that was copied from the reliable Honda CG125 and benefitting from a good seat height of 790mm that I could sit comfortably in a nice neutral stance, and on that basis, I was sold on it.

Something I shamefully left a little late, whilst worrying about what kit not to take, was raising money for charity, and as a result, I had to cram it

15

in at the last minute. I wanted to do something that would last, so I contacted Penny Appeal who takes donations and sink wells to provide clean water in developing countries. It was perfect, they were very supportive and gave me all the guidance needed, that with a Just Giving page set up, I could set off feeling at ease with the world.

Day 1 – Destination Brighton

On the first day, Brighton was the destination. My father wanted to join me on his BMW RS1200 for the first 150 miles and so we met at the local supermarket at 10am, fuelled up and set the sat nav to Brighton, it proclaiming - 265 miles in six hours and 55 minutes.

We fired the bikes in to life and headed towards London. I could hear the roar of my Dad's BMW engine behind me and as I reached my cruising speed of 55mph, the roar waned and I was sure that the only noise that was now coming from the BMW would be the sound of my father sobbing at my leisurely pace.

In the city, the air was thick with fumes and it was absolutely stifling with not a cloud in the sky. The traffic was hardly moving and we dodged and wove though the traffic jams trying to keep the air moving through our jackets. Finally, when we could take no more, we pulled into a grimy garage near Bexleyheath, gasping for a cold drink. We had planned to make the days' main stop at Ramsgate, so with our thirsts quenched, we ploughed on and a hour and 10 minutes later, I was joyfully lapping at a cracking Turkish Delight ice cream from a little ice cream parlour called Sorbetto, with a cool breeze on my face, overlooking the boats bobbing up and down in the harbour.

Fully refreshed and cooled, we rode on to Dover, where I said my farewells to my father and I trekked on alone, though Folkestone, Hastings and into Brighton and, nearly nine hours after leaving, I rolled on to the grounds of a very basic campsite, but with a nice clean shower block and an old school coke machine and at a cost of only £11 per night.

I pitched my tent and grabbed a coke which I slovenly drank in shower in my rush to get to the town to quench my hunger pangs, where all types of goodies were surely awaiting me. I parked my bike in a motorcycle bay next to Brighton's iconic Palace Pier, pulled off my helmet and was instantly hit by the energy, colour, wild clothing and the amount of people on roller skates! I wandered into town with my stomach now groaning loudly for food and after a short walk, I found a little place called Casa Della Pizza, an all you can eat buffet type of affair. The food was great with pizza, pasta, chicken and salad all passing my lips. I rolled out several pounds heavier and feeling pleased with myself as it cost less than a tenner.

I started to walk back to my bike with the aim of heading back to the campsite, but on seeing a rather packed glass fronted bar close to the sea front, full of life with people cheering and having fun, I felt it would be rude not to toast the success of the first day and my arrival in Brighton.

I squeezed in and fought my way to the bar to order a beer and as I did, the cheering grew louder and louder. The barman slopped my drink across the bar, and as I picked it up, wiping the bottom of the glass along the drip mat, a gap in the crowd appeared and I could see a pair of long legs in fishnet tights and a slinky black mini skirt, twerking at the audience. My curiosity grew and I drew closer, squeezing in deeper through the crowd, spilling more beer to get a better look at the energetic figure pulsating on the dance floor. As I drew near and with a sudden jerk of her hips, she spun around and in an instant, the bearded wonder facing me shimmy shock my delusion away and I retreated back to the bar laughing as the amazingly brilliant act began to strip layers and fling them into the audience, much to the joy of the cheering crowd, and as I stood watching, I knew my journey had truly begun.

I loved Brighton; the town is so full of life. Highlights for me were standing on the pier watching the liberal and diverse array of people wandering around, standing outside the Royal Pavilion, where my mind was taken to faraway lands and heading down The Lanes where I wandered down the winding passageways of cafes, pubs, restaurants and shops, soaking up the atmosphere and watching people having a thoroughly good time.

Day 2 – Brighton to Looe

In the morning I woke early, packed up my gear and tightened the chain on my bike, setting the routine for the coming days. I set the sat nav on my phone for Looe in Cornwall, popped it into its holder and fired up the little bike's engine, opened the throttle, said goodbye to Brighton and headed for Cornwall.

I rode through Portsmouth and on to Torquay, stopping for a drink and to stretch my legs. As I rode, I was in total awe of the seemingly never-ending conveyer belt of natural features: sandy beaches; impressive cliffs with sheer drops to the sea; and lazy estuaries, until I rolled on to the campsite.

On arrival at the campsite, the owner greeted me with *"So you're on your own aye?"* with a high twang at the end of the sentence, *"Let me see"* he said, *"Ah number 28, I think that's about the furthest away from the play area we can get ya"* then after a short pause, he snapped *"It'll be quieter for ya, we only sell takeaway, but you can eat it in the bar".* *"No bar meals then?"* I said jovially, *"Nope, sorry",* he replied, not even looking up from his paperwork. Bemused and amused, I pitched my tent in plot number 28, and after taking the panniers off, I yobishly caned the bike back down the hills and winding roads into Looe's harbour, in search of food.

I parked up in one of the many bike spaces in a car park, which I found next to the bustling main street, the main business of which, clearly being tourism. Much of the main street featured hotels, guest houses, pubs, restaurants and shops with beach equipment hanging from their doors, interspersed with ice cream and Cornish pasty vendors.

Looe at its heart, defiantly remains a fishing town and has retained several fish sellers on the east side of the Quay. This, I decided, was where I would like to sit and eat, so I wandered into the first "award winning" pasty shop and purchased a large steak and blue cheese pasty and a cup of tea to go, for the princely sum of one pound, as the shop was shutting for the day. I headed for the harbour side to watch the boats bob up and down and eat my fill.

On arrival, I was disappointed at the sight of all the backs of heads gazing out from the benches and all seemed lost until I spotted a free seat, tucked away at the end. The bench contained a solitary lady who seemed to be staring at the floor and before it was taken by another person, I hurried over and slid on to the end, banging into the feet of a breast feeding four year old who must have jumped as the mother winced. Now unsure of protocol, I apologised to the disgruntled pair and turned to sit with my back to them and stuffed my face too.

I rode back down the hills at a sedate pace to the campsite, grabbed my action camera from the tent and headed for the bar to charge it. On entry my eyes scanned the 1970s décor for a power socket and I found one spare socket next to the fruit machine. I plugged in my camera to charge it and when I looked up, six blokes perched on stools at the bar with the owner, who was now on bar duty and all of them now staring at me, like I had interrupted their caravan club meeting. "Hello lads", I shouted way too loudly and with a few grunts and nods they went back to their meeting and I ordered a pint, charged my gear and kicked back for an hour before retreating to my tent.

For me, the highlight of Looe is its harbour, a great place to sit for a while, looking out to sea, the life blood of the town. When you are there, eat local treats, there is food on offer on every street corner, in my opinion, not eating a pasty in Looe would be sacrilege! The offering of fillings is vast from the traditional to the succulent steak and blue Cheese to a spicy Chickpea Curry, and if you finished the night at a pub with a plate of white bait and a pint of a local dark ale you would not have gone far wrong.

Day 3 – Looe to Lynton, via Land's End

Setting off from the campsite in Looe early in the morning, the sun was shining and my mood was good. As I rode through St Austel, l I felt I was getting into my riding stride and breezed through Helston and to the last stretch of the A30 to Land's End and there I could see the queuing traffic for the car park. Feeling that queue jumping may be frowned upon, I pulled up to wait my turn behind an old yellow VW camper van that was burning fuel so inefficiently, I could taste the petrol in the sooty fumes. The heat of day was again incredible and I was not only being punished from the sun but also from the little air-cooled engine as the heat permeated up though my body. After what seemed like ages, I could take no more and I pulled away, passing the queuing cars. I saw a parking attendant in the car park and I pulled up beside him and said "sorry, got to get this gear off I'm dying of heat exhaustion!" – "Park around the back", he shouted back.

As I pulled up, there were only two other motor-cycles, one with a couple from Scotland loading up their big adventure bike, her in her early 20s and he in his 30s. The girl had a positive outlook, she owned a CB125 and was taking her full bike test, she was interested in my trip. The chap was nice, if a little pessimistic. He told me that Glasgow was dangerous and warned me that I could be pushed off my bike and have it stolen. I glanced over to my little Chinese 125 thinking how unlikely anyone would want it, but just smiled back as he said that he could ask about a bike locker for me, as his mate owned the company. I thanked him, took the details down and said farewell.

The other bike was a GPZ and the owner, who I met on my return, was a chef or rather an ex-chef as he had just been let go from his job and he was suffering with a heart condition from a heart attack the previous year. The poor chap was in a state and I got to be his counsellor for about 40 minutes, smiling and nodding, hopefully in all the right places!

As I stood there looking out across the steep cliff faces of 250 million year old granite rocks that are so hard and weather resistant, I realised that the scene would not have changed for the mere 300 years that visitors have been paying homage to the end of the land. This was in steep contrast to the bedlam of performing pirates and music booming over my shoulder behind me.

Until quite recently, Land's End was in the owner-ship of a Cornish family, but in the end, it fell into the hands of a businessman, who outbid the National Trust to purchase it for nearly £7 million in 2012. Immediately, he set about increasing the development, ensuring that the captive audience has plenty of over priced merchandise, food and drinks for all of the demanding children and reluctant parents. Having said that, however, it is still a must see and has some spectacular scenery!

After seeing all that Land's End had to offer, I rode to the Sunny Lyn campsite in Lynton, where Exmoor meets the sea. The roads were tight and winding and featured some of the steepest hills that I had ever ridden on my 125cc. Going up the hills, the engine and clutch smelt like they were going to ignite at any moment and going down them, the brakes did the same, but it was well worth it, as I was greeted by a campsite set in a gorge with a river running though it and a pub serving oriental food and real ale; a match made in heaven.

The day had been enjoyable, Lands' End is obviously a must, but to dwell there for more than an hour is a bit of a waste, in my opinion. I was glad that I had headed to Lynton early enough to see all that it had to offer. I would highly recommend taking a walk to see the gorge and take in the air. The air seems to be so clean, I guess it's because of all of the trees and because it is trapped in the valley. The locally produced food which I sampled was fantastic, I highly recommend trying the locally produced high-quality beef, cheeses and vegetables, I am sure that if you try any of these, however delivered to you on the plate, you will not be disappointed.

Day 4 - Lynton to Tenby

Setting off from Lynton, I was looking forward to meeting up with an old friend, David, for a coffee in Minehead. I had been looking forward to this part of the trip as David would join me on my journey on his GSX-R 600 up the A39 to Bridgwater in Somerset. It was great to have someone ride with me for a short while, supporting me along the way.

Riding up towards Trevayne Farm campsite in Tenby, Pembrokeshire, the landscape changed significantly. Leaving behind the South Coast, the north seemed to be wilder and more rugged with sheer, sharp looking cliffs, flanked by the Atlantic Ocean. That night, the prevailing north-westerly winds hit the coast perfectly, brought in by the low-pressure weather conditions that had moved in from the Atlantic and spots of rain started to fall as I found my way on to the campsite. It was almost strange to see the rain fall as we had not seen any rain for what seemed like months, due to the heatwave which we had been experiencing.

I unpacked my panniers and pitched my tent a little way back from the cliff, as all the prime spaces had been taken. I walked through the farm to the shower block which was covered by a tin roof and as I started to shower, the heavens opened for about five minutes. The noise was deafening as the rain hit the tin roof, it sounding more like nails thumping on the metal, giving an exciting almost apocalyptic feel and then in a heartbeat, the rain stopped leaving me in an almost perfect silence.

Refreshed from my shower, I rode into another picturesque town. Tenby is a walled seaside town that has a lot to offer, and in stark contrast to the sedate Lynton, it is busy and full of life, I would recommend a wander to see the Five Arches Gate, a large tower which was built in the mid-16th century and take in its history, then hit the town and enjoy the atmosphere!

I ate pizza in a little café called Get Stuffed and raced back to the tent, fearing a soaking and not wanting to have to deal with wet clothing. I arrived back at the tent, crawled in and fell asleep almost instantly, exhausted by the day's riding, only to be woken at 2am by screaming children and my tent listing in the wind. I unzipped my tent to see a dozen silhouettes of people running around screaming commands to each other as they packed their kids into their cars and fought to hold their tents down. Luckily for me, their cars and my bike on its side stand next to the tent, took the brunt of the wind and I even managed to get a couple more hours' sleep.

I awoke in the morning to find the other campers gathering their scattered belongings and packing their cars. I too packed up my gear, checked the chain and oil, set the sat nav for Llanberis in North Wales and rolled back down the farm track to find fuel and coffee, that both came by way of the Five Ways Garage, a humorously miserable little garage with a cashier that managed to stare at me briefly, take my money, and not say a single word, so I thanked her for her company and told her if she wished to chat more, I would be drinking my coffee on the forecourt!

Day 5 - Tenby to Llanberis

Wales never lets me down, it always rains! It's not like rain that we get at home in Suffolk, it's Welsh rain, a light constant rain that seems to hold more water than it heavier counterparts and it reduces your visibility like fog, if ever there was a rain that was out to get you then it would be Welsh rain!

Wales holds a special place in my heart, it's a place that I have spent lots of time in. I love the rugged coastal cliffs that project harshly from wide soft sandy beaches and dunes creating some of the most beautiful landscapes and in my opinion, a visit to the Gower Peninsula should be undertaken by all.

As I rode into the mountains, the rain relentlessly bore down, running down to the small lakes, swelling the rivers and streams, turning them from sedate to raging torrents of white water. Even the roads began to fill as I powered on to Llanberis where I had booked a bed in dormitory at an old climbing haunt called Pete's Eats - a cafe and bunk house, with hot showers, a map room and big plates of food and tea by the pint.

As I climbed up the pass towards Snowdon, the bike seemed to be struggling in the rain, as was I, I was soaked to the bone and my arse was killing. The bike spluttered and puttered as we hit the pinnacle of the pass next to the Pen-Y-Pass car park, and just as the road started on the long steep decent down to Llanberis, a KTM 390 Duke pumped past me and I was having none of it. The road was steep, and I was rolling fast - this wasn't going to be about engine size, this was going to be about the size of the brass. I flew up behind him with no idea of the speed because the clocks had misted over on the inside. We weaved in and out of the cars, ploughing through the water like jet skis and, without warning, the back end slipped out and I struggled to hold it up as I skidded into a layby and watched the duke disappear into the rain, probably off to pick up an extra tin of Brasso!

I pulled up at Pete's Eats, checked in and was given a small parking spot by the kitchen door. I headed straight for the drying room and filled it with my wet belongings. Then threw the rest of my gear in the room that I managed to have to myself as the couple that had booked it, had not turned up. I went downstairs and there I ate a monster omelette and drunk two pints of tea. After I had my fill, I swiftly retreated to my room to lay face down for a short while as sitting on the wooden seating was becoming a tad uncomfortable!

There is much to do in Llanberis but as I was only there for one night, I had to make do with a cone of salty chips that I did not need and a walk to take in my surroundings and sit by a lake edged by mountains. If time and the weather permits, get up in the mountains, the way to do this by burning less time and the least amount of calories is to take the Snowdon Mountain Railway up Snowdon, from the last stop it is just a short, but steep walk, to the summit. I love to sit and look out at Lake Padarn and Vivien Quarry is well worth a look too. It is always good to mingle with the mountaineers and adventure seekers, resting and refuelling at Pete's Eats with a statutory pint of tea.

Day 6 – Llanberis to Kendal

In the morning it was still pouring down with rain. Thankfully my clothes had dried overnight and with my waterproofs donned, I hit the road for the historic market town of Kendal.

I rode up to Liverpool, and as I approached the Forest of Bowland, the sun started to beat down again and in no time, I and the little bike were as dry as a bone. It was the shortest ride of the trip at just under five hours, with a halfway rest and an opportunity to change the oil and fix a couple of minor issues with the bike.

I was fortunate to have a couple of hours to explore Kendal, it is steeped in history and is a polite, well turned out town with art galleries, town houses with architectural appeal and attractive churches. I paid a visit to one of its pubs for a meal with a Cumberland sausage and a huge bowl of sticky toffee pudding – delicious! If you get a chance, sample the local food on offer, it's very good.

The accommodation was fantastic, called the Kendal Hostel, set in a Georgian town house with the Brewery Arts Centre just 150 yards away. The family-run hostel is a friendly home-from-home with a comfortable lounge, free Wi-Fi, a well-equipped kitchen, dining room, laundry facilities, a drying room and great beds. It is a great place to stop to break-up any journey to and from Scotland, as well as being a great base to explore this beautiful part of the country. I spent a very comfortable night and had a great sleep, which set me up for the next days' riding.

Day 7 – Kendal to Fort William and Loch Linnhe

As I rode towards Fort William, the Scottish roads

were amazing, not cluttered with junctions, but long and winding passes through some of most spectacular mountains, pine forests and mystical wetland valleys. The landscape was changing, more rugged almost ominous but enchanting and beautiful, somewhere magic would almost seem possible.

As rode up towards Glasgow I needed fuel, the finest high-octane unleaded for my bike and a strong coffee for me. I pulled in to a garage, one of those ones with a Subway inside. I filled my bike, paid for the fuel and walked over to the Subway counter, "black coffee please" I proclaimed to the pierced and punky looking pair behind the counter that looked like they had just fallen out of bed. "We don't do coffee, there's a costa machine" with a grubby hand stretched out pointing across the shop to a grimy looking machine. "Sorry that's' city coffee chap, you know a lighter roast", I was getting more and more English by the second, and their dead pan faces just stared almost through me, "See I like French coffee, a darker roast" and with that the pair looked at each other then back at me roared uncontrollably with laughter, "coffee's coffee", the girl said, "to you it might be" I said and I walked out to the sound of their sniggering - Welcome to Glasgow, I thought!

For my first night in Scotland, I pitched my tent on the edge of the stunning Loch Linnhe, this I thought was the perfect spot and ate potato cakes and beans from the can, which I had grabbed from the campsite's shop.

Day 8 – Loch Linnhe to Helmsdale via John O'Groats

In the morning, I woke early and sat on the shore and ate cold potato cakes. I packed my bike and wheeled it out so not to wake the other campers. I rode the short distance into Fort William for a coffee and to top up my tank, ready to push on up towards John O'Groats.

On the way, and not knowing what to expect at John O'Groats, I seized the opportunity and swung in to the car park of a German supermarket so that I could resupply myself with some cans of cold milky coffee, some fresh bread, cheese and a half bottle of red wine to celebrate the impending victory of bagging John O'Groats that evening and merrily fall asleep in my tent listening to the ocean.

As I rode up the road to John O'Groats, a place that I had intended to camp, I felt a massive sense of achievement. This was sharply followed by a strange and sudden emptying of my soul and a slight feeling of desolation. It may have been due to the "the end of the road" sign on display, half a mile before. It may have been simply just knowing that I was getting closer to the end of my journey or it may have been the exhaustion from the nine hours' riding that I had endured, but by an amazing piece of luck, my phone rang and to my joy it was a kindly offer of a free night's stay at a B&B in Helmsdale, Sutherland, and even though it was over an hours' ride away, I jumped at the offer to escape my now dark trophy of John O' Groats.

The additional hour in the saddle was compensated by an amazing ride and views of the Scottish coast that ran all the way down the stretch of the A9, all the way to the doorstep of the B&B - a large 1930s white semi-detached nestled into the landscape at the side of the road, overlooking the sea.

On arrival, the owner, a slight, pock faced man from Germany had kindly made space in his lean-to at the side of the house to overnight my bike, keeping it safe and dry.

I was shown to my room, the cold of the day seemed to be deep in my bones and I had to listen hard to get each word as he told me the rules in an almost bullet point fashion from his pre composed speech.

As he talked, I looked around the room, it was strangely decorated with dark wood panelling and pictures of dolls on the walls which gave it a slightly eerie feeling. I then realised that the owner had finished his well-rehearsed spiel and that he was standing awkwardly in the door way, reluctantly making small talk to bridge my lack of response or to up his trip advisor ratings. I struggled to talk and all I wanted to do was fall on to the bed, get warm and sleep in the comfort, but with one last push, I snapped back in to life and reassured him I would not be back after midnight, as I would not be going out, and that scrambled eggs instead of fried would be fantastic. I apologised and forced myself reluctantly out of the door to shake him off and get to the bike to tighten my chain. I wasted no time to get straight back to my room, turned up the electric heaters and jumped into shower in an attempt to drive the cold from my body. I dried myself, fell on to the bed and lay there, eating my bread and cheese, intermittently washing it down with the red wine. After a good nights' sleep and a mighty breakfast, I was rejuvenated and bursting with energy for the rest of the journey ahead.

Scottish Offerings

One of the mistakes I made, was not allowing more time in Scotland. An extra day or two may have given me the time I needed to take more in, I pushed too hard in Scotland, this was not due to the speed of my bike, on the whole it was not an issue on the Scottish roads and I would often be held up by a car, lorry or most of all a campervan with their chilled out free-spirited drivers, great people to chat to at the campsite but a pain in the arse to get stuck behind as I didn't quite have the grunt to safely get past before the next bend!

If I had had more time, I would have liked to explore the cities and castles, and maybe to have pushed on to Skye, a place that I have since visited and loved every minute of it.

For me, whilst on the road, I always try to call into a proper local bakery. I have never regretted it, no matter what part of the country I am in, I try not to pass one!

In Scotland, one of the nicest things that I ate, next their truly word class seafood, was a small pie with a pastry crust filled with a haggis type mix in the bottom and mashed potatoes on the top. It was real soul food, something I believe is called a Meat and Tattie pie, they are amazing. They can be filled with a peppery lamb or beef, with a raised pie crust that can sometimes optionally be filled mushy peas. I highly recommend them, that and the seafood!

Day 9 - Helmsdale to Berwick-upon-Tweed

Every now and then on the road, and prolific on that stretch of the A9, I would see a giant bike chug past me, with what could only be described as three custom-made shipping containers bolted on, topped with an array of dry bags, one strapped on top of the other, wobbling past like the Beverly Hillbillies, a quick hand up and slap back down, as they passed me on the long roads. When encountering traffic jams, they lost the gyroscopic action of their wheels that had been holding them up and I would nip back past them, or wave my condolences at them in the petrol stations, with my near 100 miles per gallon on my side. Sometimes I would stop and have a chat, and found that they always gave good advice and great encouragement and I would gaze slightly enviously at all the gadgets and luxuries that they had.

Like with my friend David, a few times on the journey, people would ride with me for a while, at times making me feel a little like Forrest Gump and I probably pushed the bike a little harder than I should have out of speed shame. They rode with me until they were picked off by boredom and with a quick thumbs up and a thump of their engines, they would be gone.

I set off early after a hearty breakfast and while I rode, I contemplated the longest day of the trip and my mind again turned to the people that thought it was it was crazy to do it on a 125 and insane to do it on a Chinese one at that. I think the automatic assumption of the downside of taking a 125cc machine on such a long journey would be speed, and sitting at 55 mph, dropping down to less than 30 mph on the steep hills, it could be a little embarrassing. However, on the whole, the speed issues would slip away and a different mind-set would kick in, becoming just me and the road. On the long stretches, I had time to see the detail in the scenery, with time to think and to get things straight, then on hitting some of the fantastic winding roads I encountered, I had the joy of pushing the little machine to its limits and to be honest, I found it all quite therapeutic and enjoyable, though that said, it wasn't all song and sunshine, there were dark, dark, days.

The little bike had its problems that caused me concern as to its reliability. It spat out an oil seal that had been nipped whilst on the production line, which I replaced with a O ring from a tap washer kit of the same size. The little Chinese machine's electrics did not see the Welsh rain coming and the clocks fogged over and the engine spat, but the Lake District dried them out again and we moved on with the help of a can of spray oil. Scotland undone its rear sprocket, and that was very nearly the undoing of me! The chain stretched out like an elastic band with its little knock-off copy engine keeping me in a constant state of anxiety, but it did its job and plodded on, as they do now. I believe that, on whole, with the borrowed engine technology used by some Chinese motorcycle companies, the engines are reasonably reliable, the real hurdle is getting the rest of the bike to cope with the British weather.

As I rode on the rain came down again, hard, and without my knowledge, my waterproof trousers had risen up and the tongues of my boots was greedily funnelling the water in. I pulled into a McDonalds at Berwick-upon-Tweed on the A1, sloshed through to the toilet and in the cubicle, I took off my boots and poured the contents down the toilet and sighed at my stupidity. With that I heard a "come on son, we had better find another toilet, I think he's sick" I didn't have the energy to call out and explain. Now out of my waterproofs, I ordered two meals, both with coffee, to try to pull myself back into life.

I had planned to camp in the North York Moors at Robin Hood's Bay, but had booked myself into another B&B, at a farmhouse in order to have a chance to dry my boots out. On arrival, they had no idea I was coming as it was booked via an online broker. They left me standing in the rain, bags in hand for

10 minutes while they confirmed my booking, then apologised for keeping me waiting.

Once I had been verified, they kindly let me in out of the pouring rain and they let me dry my gear in their boiler. I ensured that I got my money's worth by laying in their jacuzzi for two hours, easing my aching muscles and warming through thoroughly. I then crawled in to bed and slept like a log.

Day 10 – Berwick-upon-Tweed to home

In the morning I came downstairs to be pointed towards a full English breakfast, that was already awaiting me on the table, with no prior arrangement. Luckily I'm not Jewish or a vegetarian, but it may have been okay if I was a horse, as it had a small amount of grass cooked in with the egg! I pushed it around the plate, eating the marmalade and toast with the coffee and steathily feeding the rest to the owner's greedy black Labrador, that nearly had my arm off trying to gobble it down as fast as it could before we got caught.

Luckily, for the rest of the journey down the east coast, it remained hot, sunny and dry with a great run down through Newcastle and I really enjoyed riding through the historical and industrial land-scapes, through the North York Moors and into Robin Hood's Bay where I enjoyed a piece of fish and a strong black coffee.

The North York Moors are a fantastic place to visit, a wild and rugged plateau with impressive valleys (dales) that cut deeply in to the earth. The whole wind-swept area is bursting with wildlife such as dear, ponies and rear breed sheep, running wild, giving a slightly Mongolian/Wild West feeling with endless possibilities of adventure.

For me a trip to Robin Hood's Bay, was a must, it is a place that my father sheltered in February 1989 in his ship, the St Nicola from a raging storm that had hit his ship, with gusts recorded 146 mph. He often spoke about it and I was keen to pay a visit.

I pressed on down to Grimsby and through Boston, when with a bang, the chain was off. Luckily it had just came off the rear sprocket, but it had stretched so much that it no longer fitted the sprocket properly, something that I knew I should have replaced with a heavy-duty O-ring chain, but it would have to do and I would just have to be a little more ginger with it until I got to King's Lynn where I would revaluate.

I considered staying overnight in King's Lynn, but with only a short stint around the coast of East Anglia left, I tightened the chain some more and grinded on, pushing in the extra four and a half hours with the lure of my own bed.

10 days, and 3,327 miles later, I rolled back up my driveway, bruised and battered but I had an amazing sense of achievement, and an overwhelming gratitude to all the great people that I met along the journey and the donations given to The Penny Appeal for drinking water wells in developing countries.

Lessons Learnt

Doing the British Coast in 10 days, spending up to 12½ hours a day in the saddle on a 125, was an adventure and test of endurance that gave me joy in the sense of achievement. A bigger bike would have joyously got me past those loveable campervans, and doing the journey in campervan would kept me warm and dry with a good night's sleep.

But no matter the transportation, giving myself 14 days to complete the just over 3000 mile journey, would have certainly given me more time to enjoy the land, the food and people and with a little less fatigue.

Also, as much as I love camping, hostels may have offered more advantages and they are extremely cost effective, often have single and double rooms too and have cooking, clothes washing and drying facilities. However, I'm sure there are those that will complete the journey in less days than me on a smaller bike and camp all the way. But for everyone that completes the best road trip adventure the UK has to offer, I tip my hat to you and welcome you to the club.

With great thanks to everyone
that donated money that helped
change lives forever.

Printed in Great Britain
by Amazon